IN THE
NATIONAL INTEREST

General Sir John Monash once exhorted a graduating class to 'equip yourself for life, not solely for your own benefit but for the benefit of the whole community'. At the university established in his name, we repeat this statement to our own graduating classes, to acknowledge how important it is that common or public good flows from education.

Universities spread and build on the knowledge they acquire through scholarship in many ways, well beyond the transmission of this learning through education. It is a necessary part of a university's role to debate its findings, not only with other researchers and scholars, but also with the broader community in which it resides.

Publishing for the benefit of society is an important part of a university's commitment to free intellectual inquiry. A university provides civil space for such inquiry by its scholars, as well as for investigations by public intellectuals and expert practitioners.

This series, In the National Interest, embodies Monash University's mission to extend knowledge and encourage informed debate about matters of great significance to Australia's future.

Professor Margaret Gardner AC
President and Vice-Chancellor,
Monash University

RICHARD MARLES

TIDES THAT BIND: AUSTRALIA IN THE PACIFIC

MONASH
UNIVERSITY
PUBLISHING

Monash University Publishing
Matheson Library Annexe
40 Exhibition Walk
Monash University
Clayton, Victoria 3800, Australia
https://publishing.monash.edu

Monash University Publishing brings to the world publications which advance the best traditions of humane and enlightened thought.

ISBN: 9781922464590 (paperback)
ISBN: 9781922464606 (ebook)

Series: In the National Interest
Editor: Louise Adler
Project manager & copyeditor: Paul Smitz
Designer: Peter Long
Typesetter: Cannon Typesetting
Proofreader: Gillian Armitage
Printed in Australia by Ligare Book Printers

A catalogue record for this book is available from the National Library of Australia.

To the peoples and leaders of the Pacific, in gratitude
for their warmth, friendship and kindness.

TIDES THAT BIND: AUSTRALIA IN THE PACIFIC

In the nondescript hall, with a sea breeze providing only a modicum of relief from the stifling heat, discomfort remained our host. There were no seats, just a bare floor. And for my middle-aged body, which has the innate flexibility of a crowbar, sitting cross-legged for any period was a mild form of torture.

I was worried for my companion, too. Despite the then governor-general's unflappable grace, sitting on the floor in her immaculate attire was definitely not in the handbook. And if my aching bones were any guide, there had to be a limit to what could be asked of the vice-regal limbs. So I suggested to her that I find a chair.

But Quentin Bryce is complete class. She wouldn't hear of it. The most senior of the Tuvaluan women were sitting on the floor and so would she. This moment was not about her, it was about the kids who were ready to perform, and she was hardly going to steal their limelight by being the only person perched on a chair. And so we sat and watched and listened as teams of children took their turns in dance and song.

With expectations set at what an equivalent cohort of pre-teens might offer in Melbourne or Brisbane, what emanated was simply angelic. The mood of the room changed instantly. Our senses were elevated to a heavenly place by the purity of the voices and the precision of the harmony. The dancing was elegant, captivating and joyful.

What we were seeing was amazing. In this unremarkable hall, on Funafuti atoll in the small island nation of Tuvalu in the middle of the Pacific—remote, distant—we had happened upon the indescribable. The tiny population of about 5000 had produced a performance worthy of New York's Carnegie Hall or London's Royal Albert Hall.

The governor-general was as astounded as I was. Stiff, cramping legs were irrelevant. This was a moment to behold, and we were privileged to witness it.

Just as on that day in March 2012 in Tuvalu, from 2010 to 2013 I was honoured to experience the character and generosity of Pacific culture and society time and again as I travelled this extraordinary region while serving as Australia's parliamentary secretary for Pacific island affairs.

LOVE AT FIRST SIGHT

My first encounter with the Pacific occurred in 1984 when I visited Papua New Guinea on a Geelong Grammar School trip. After one night in Port Moresby, we touched down on a grass airstrip at Simbai in the highlands of Madang Province. The local community had donned their traditional costumes and face paint, and a sing-sing greeted us at the plane and accompanied us as we walked to the village hall. I can still remember my senses being overwhelmed by the vibrant colours, tribal sounds and rare smells. For a fresh-faced sixteen-year-old from a cloistered environment in Geelong, this was an unimaginably exotic experience, one that sparked inside me an affection that would only grow over time and extend across the Pacific.

A few days later, as we hiked through the mountains, damage from a storm forced us onto a route which clearly had not been walked by visitors in years. Before long, we were deep in the jungle, many hours' walk from the nearest settlement and an entire world away from our comfort zones. And then, in the depths of this wilderness, we came across a local couple living alone in a small hut. Our surprise at seeing them was nothing compared with their complete astonishment at a passing parade of a dozen young white people—we may as well have descended from Mars. Our guides from Simbai and the couple did not seem to share any of Papua New Guinea's 832 languages, and yet in no time at all, through a combination of sign language and the odd comprehensible word, the man of the house agreed to guide us to the next village, a twelve-hour return walk. (His service proved invaluable, which later begged the question: what on earth was the plan had we not run into him?)

Towards the end of a long day, our new friend began calling into the mountains. And soon there was a reply. This was the highlands way of ringing ahead to let the tiny hamlet of Tsarap know that it was about to receive a visit, the likes of which it had never had before. As we approached, a group of children ran out as a spontaneous greeting party and walked the last stretch with us. The younger kids followed tentatively, gently touching our skin. And as two peoples unexpectedly came face to face, once again we were met with the Pacific hospitality we were quickly growing accustomed to. We slept that night on the floor of the village hall, after swapping the food we carried with that offered by the warm folk of Tsarap.

We had been away from Australia for less than a week and already my world had exploded in size. Here in Papua New Guinea, life was being lived in a way that I had never seen before. And thirty-seven years later, having since travelled far and wide from Geelong, I now know that PNG life is lived in a way unlike anywhere else in the world. In 1984, my understanding of how astounding are these lives was only just beginning. But already, for me, it was love at first sight. Papua New Guinea—dubbed the Land of the Unexpected—was simply incredible, and it remains so today.

PROTECTING PACIFIC CULTURE

The Pacific truly is a place of wonder.

On a map of human density, China and India are at the heart of the world's population, and Europe, the Americas and Africa follow, whereas the Pacific encompasses many of the smallest communities, those most remote from the centre. And with this remoteness comes intimacy and uniqueness.

Pacific life is unencumbered by the smorgasbord of distractions facing those of us in dense habitation. Human creativity and generosity are remarkable here, as expressed by the beauty of the local cultures and the social norms of the people. The way in which the islanders present their view of the world through art is different, as are the materials used to achieve this. Tapa—cloth made from beaten bark—is their canvas, and its distinctive texture yields the unmistakable signature of Pacific craft.

Often, music is simply unaccompanied voices formed into harmonic choirs. But in Papua New Guinea's Bougainville region, instruments comprise hollow lengths of bamboo beaten by the wielder on one end, usually with an old thong. The length of the bamboo determines the note. More than a dozen bamboo tubes are played by a single musician, and in turn entire orchestras of players produce novel versions of pop songs, national anthems and even classical music.

Dance is a birthright: it appears that everyone can do it. The type of dance changes subtly from one country and region to another. There is an ornateness to dance here which can be lost on the outsider, but its beauty certainly isn't. The haka—the familiar Māori challenge—bears witness to both the historical existence of war and a contemporary warrior culture, and versions of it exist throughout the Pacific.

The inhabitants of atolls such as those in Tuvalu, the Marshall Islands and Kiribati have an innate connection with the sea. The ocean is a source of comfort and security, of food, play and culture. The way the water moves, and the stars arrayed above it, are also tools of navigation, as you can learn from the Marshallese.

Families, tribes and clans across the Pacific are organised in distinctive ways. Reciprocity is the obligation to make an offering when asking for any kind of favour. It is a deeply felt concept which drives standards of behaviour that, all too often, Western sensibilities fail to understand. In Australia, stereotypes abound with respect to 'Pacific time', the framing of people from the region as unmotivated and uncommitted to work. But the perception that Pacific peoples do not take work, or education, or good governance seriously is ignorant in the extreme.

In 2011 I visited the HIV/AIDS ward at the Port Moresby Hospital—98 per cent of Pacific cases of this disease occur in Papua New Guinea.[1] There, I saw people in pain, lying on beds from which they would never rise. It was confronting and distressing. Alongside the patients were their closest family members: husband, wife, sibling, parent, child. These people were with their loved one for every moment of this final journey. Their swags were rolled up under the patient's bed, to be unfurled each night. These companions would not allow a single second of loneliness to occur. In turn, the immediate companions were supported by extended family members with food and supplies. The commitment was herculean.

And yet it was not, because this *is* life: profound, intense and completely meaningful. Here was a fierce motivation rooted in commitment to family and the dignity of life that is every bit as significant and noble as any of the values we hold dear in Australia. The truth is that the people of the Pacific are as motivated by their culture as we are by ours. The myths persist because of a failure to understand the Pacific way of life. And that failure is all too often born of an unwillingness on our part to learn.

This must change.

Globalisation is wonderful in the way in which it has cross-pollinated human development. Of course, the Pacific can, and should, benefit from this as well. But it is kinship to the lands and seas, and a deep connection among people, which has preserved the humanity that is distinct to the Pacific—a humanity the world should cherish.

Indeed, as with all cultures, that of the Pacific, and all the beauty and uniqueness which surrounds it, is a critical part of the heritage of humanity. The world would be a lesser place without it, and so it must be protected. But this plea has a deeper resonance in the Pacific compared with most other places, because the Pacific is under threat.

The region performed worst against the United Nations' Millennium Development Goals (MDGs)—a set of eight relative social measures tracked between the years 2000 and 2015—than any other part of the world. It means that development is occurring at a slower rate there compared with anywhere else. Soon, if nothing changes, the Pacific will be—in absolute terms—the least developed part of the globe. And added to this is the menacing threat of climate change. Countries like Kiribati are confronting the sobering prospect of whole islands becoming uninhabitable due to rising sea levels.

Now, more than ever, the Pacific needs a champion. The Pacific desperately wants Australia to assume this role. The rest of the world expects it of us. We need to expect it of ourselves.

In Australia, we have great Pacific expertise. We have the economy, governance, assets, affinity and international support to make a difference. The only issue standing in the way is our own willingness to embrace our international identity as leaders and in doing so fulfil our destiny.

It is time that we find both our voice and our purpose to act.

AUSTRALIA HAS HISTORY IN THE PACIFIC

Australia has a long and significant history in the Pacific. The framers of our own constitution understood that the Pacific has a special place in Australia's relationship with the world.

Subsection 51(xxix) of the Australian Constitution provides the federal parliament with the power to 'make laws ... with respect to: external affairs'. This is the constitutional power which allows our national government to manage foreign affairs; it is both well known and well understood. Less well known is subsection 51(xxx), which empowers the federal parliament to 'make laws ... with respect to: the relations of the Commonwealth with the islands of the Pacific'.

This provision was discussed during the 1898 Australasian Federation Conference. On 21 January that year, Edmund Barton—the man who would become our nation's first prime minister—said:

> It has been suggested that this sub-section is embraced in the preceding one: 'External affairs and treaties'. That is arguable; it is quite possible that it may be true; but there are a very large number of people who look forward with interest to the Commonwealth undertaking, as far as it can as part of the British Empire, the regulation of the Pacific Islands. It may be, I think, as there is a doubt as to whether the one thing is included in the other, and as there are a large number of people who are interested in this question, that it is better in deference to their views to leave the words as they are.[2]

Events have moved us on. Pacific nations have asserted independence both culturally and as sovereign nations, and Australia has grown beyond playing an imperial role on behalf of Mother England as imagined in the above passage. But another idea was embodied in these words: that the relationship between Australia and the Pacific would have special significance, that it would have different and stronger terms than those between Great Britain and the Pacific. Barton was clearly identifying the pre-eminence of regional relations.

Most striking in Barton's words is the reference to the 'large number of people' who were interested in this question. That Australia's relations with the Pacific command their own constitutional power is a demonstration of how, more than a century ago, the Pacific mattered to the people of the Australian colonies and its leaders. However, by the end of the first century of our federation, this understanding of the importance of the Pacific would be lost.

Since Federation, much of our critical history has been written through military service. The national embrace of Anzac Day is testament to this. In World War II, Australia fought some of its most significant battles in the Pacific, particularly in Papua New Guinea, including iconic battles at Milne Bay,

Gona and Buna, and along the Kokoda Track. In total, 22 000 Australians served in Papua New Guinea— 7000 of them made the ultimate sacrifice on land, in the air and at sea.[3]

The Bomana War Cemetery near Port Moresby is the resting place of many of those who died. More than 3300 Australians are interred there, making it Australia's largest war cemetery. Our second-largest war cemetery is in Lae, in Papua New Guinea's Morobe Province, where a further 2400 Australians rest—1000 more than in our largest cemetery on the Western Front, in Tyne Cot, Belgium. By any measure, the war cemeteries at Lae and Bomana are sacred ground for our nation.

Today, a stunning memorial in Isurava, Oro Province stands guard over the valley leading to the village of Kokoda. At the height of the fighting in the Battle of Isurava on the Kokoda Track, private Bruce Kingsbury stormed towards the enemy, firing his Bren gun from his hip. It was a moment of inspiration that cost Kingsbury his life but changed the course of the battle. The private was posthumously awarded the Victoria Cross, one of nine won by Australians in

Papua New Guinea during World War II. Today, local villagers lovingly care for the memorial, echoing the way in which the so-called Fuzzy Wuzzy Angels saved so many diggers eight decades ago.

Kokoda, Bomana, Isurava, Lae, Rabaul—these places are of enormous importance to the Australian psyche. They serve as a reminder of the deep history we share with the Pacific and its people. But profound historical and personal connections both precede and succeed World War II. While Australia, in the aftermath of European settlement, spent more than a century as a British colony, what is not as widely remembered by Australians is that we also have a history as a colonial power. Two Pacific countries—Papua New Guinea and Nauru—spent time under the administration of Australia.

After World War I, the League of Nations dismantled the German empire. Australia, already responsible for the administration of the territory of Papua, was also given mandate over New Guinea. Apart from the period of the Japanese occupation of some of the northern parts of New Guinea during World War II, both areas remained in Australian hands until the independence of Papua New Guinea was proclaimed on 16 September 1975.

Nauru first entered Australian control in 1914 when we seized the island at the outbreak of World War I. After the war, the League of Nations granted Australia, Great Britain and New Zealand a joint mandate over Nauru. Japan then occupied Nauru from 1942 until 1945, when the United Nations decreed it a trust territory to be administered by Australia. Nauru gained its independence on 31 January 1968.

Both Papua New Guinea and Nauru maintain a significant affinity with Australia. The leaderships of both countries hold a keen interest in, and their people a real affection for, our nation. Australia has also left a cultural imprint. Many laws are derived from ours, and the systems of government are familiar. The connection even extends to sport: the National Rugby League (NRL) State of Origin matches define three of the biggest days in the PNG calendar, and Australian Rules football is the official national sport of Nauru. Furthermore, many leading figures in these nations were educated in Australia. In the case of Nauru, for a long time while it experienced significant wealth, an Australian private school education was a birthright—today, one in four Nauruans are actually Australian citizens.

With this common heritage, the ways in which Papua New Guinea and Nauru have fared since each gained independence forms a significant part of Australia's international report card. Accordingly, it is crucial that the prosperity of the peoples of both countries, and the wellbeing of their national governments, remain matters of Australia's abiding interest.

And yet they have not. The achievement of independence in both Nauru and Papua New Guinea prompted all the celebration and optimism befitting the birth of a new nation. It also should have heralded a new relationship with Australia, one in which we were no longer the administrator but a very present and supportive friend. In truth, it was the moment we left.

At the time of Papua New Guinea's independence, for example, there were approximately 50 000 Australians living there. Today there are 10 000, most of whom are FIFO (fly in, fly out) residents. National freedom saw—across government, civil society, and all the ancillary economic activities that went with them—a large-scale exodus by Australians. Some of this had to happen to make space for Papua New Guineans to take over the running of their country. But in hindsight, much of it was abandonment.

As Australians physically left the Pacific, interest in the region from government, the media and the public diminished. Stories stopped being written about Papua New Guinea. Students stopped studying the Pacific in our universities. And the government embarked on an era of being present in the Pacific, but without any intent.

In transition, Australia's new role in the Pacific was poorly defined and poorly fulfilled. We lost our way.

AT A CROSSROADS

Since my adolescent adventure in Papua New Guinea, I have visited many parts of the world. I have seen refugee camps in Africa, slums in Bangladesh. But the worst human circumstances I have ever witnessed were on the islet of Betio in South Tarawa, Kiribati.

On Betio, makeshift dwellings are tightly packed into what little land exists. Despite the absence of high-rise buildings, the population density is similar to

Hong Kong. This is a crammed human existence. Tight dirt lanes, the width of a car, wind amid the homes. Rubbish is strewn everywhere—the battle for effective waste management was lost a long time ago. Plumbing is sporadic. The electricity supply seems to have been hooked up by prioritising ingenuity, not safety.

You see a set of steps descending into a dark concrete space, a realm of desolate ruin with the unmistakable, overwhelming stench of human excrement. And yet someone lives in there. That a person could be left with this dark hole in the ground as a place to call home, challenges your understanding of the ways in which life on this planet can be led.

Conditions on Betio are appalling. The health outcomes are atrocious: the prevalence of tuberculosis is the highest in the Pacific. The overcrowding is calamitous. The impact of climate change is already disastrous. So why is the plight of Betio not instinctively understood by every member of the Australian Parliament and every person within our foreign and security policy community? I ask this because the most significant bilateral partner of Kiribati is neither China nor the United States: it is us. Kiribati's currency is the

Australian dollar. Its biggest aid partner is Australia. Ask for a beer in Kiribati and you'll be served VB.

There was a time when Betio mattered greatly. There was a time, in fact, when it was at the centre of one of the greatest struggles in world history. Seventy-eight years ago, the Battle of Tarawa saw the single biggest beach landing of World War II to that point—within a year, the lessons learned there would be applied at Normandy. Betio, which was being used by the Japanese as an air base, was the site of four horrific days of conflict in which almost 6400 people would die, and American congressional Medals of Honor would be won. Today, there still exist reminders of this crucial conflict: the rusted landing craft in the lagoon, the wreck of a tank in the village, the dilapidated concrete bunkers which now provide the saddest of homes.

To see Betio, as I last did in November 2015, is confronting. It begs many questions. And, in the process, it demands one simple answer, in clear and indefatigable terms. Betio was worth fighting for in November 1943. Australia now needs to lead a new fight for Betio, and indeed all of the Pacific.[4]

To grasp the challenges facing not just Kiribati but the entire Pacific region, it's worth looking back at the United Nations' Millennium Development Goals, which included eradicating extreme poverty and hunger, reducing child mortality, and achieving universal primary education. As the countries of the Pacific reported their progress against the MDGs, the picture that emerged was bleak, particularly, as mentioned earlier, in Papua New Guinea.

Three quarters of the Pacific's poor—two million people—were found to live in PNG.[5] But the nation spent considerably less on health care than most other Pacific countries.[6] In 2011, PNG spent only A\$60 per person on health, whereas Australia spent just under A\$6000.[7] One in five children suffered from malnutrition.[8] Of the three Pacific countries where malaria is endemic—Papua New Guinea, the Solomon Islands and Vanuatu—only PNG had failed to halt the incidence of the disease, which in turn was a leading cause of mortality for the nation. The prevalence of malaria was further exacerbated by the significant presence of HIV/AIDS. PNG was also one of only two Pacific countries which did not meet the MDG target in relation to maternal health.[9] Forty-eight per cent of local women were giving birth outside of health facilities.[10]

In the Pacific, only the Cook Islands and Niue, both countries with strong relations with New Zealand, achieved all the MDGs—Kiribati, Papua New Guinea and the Solomons achieved none. By contrast, the entire African continent was on track to reach three critical MDGs: universal primary education, gender equality, and the successful combatting of HIV/AIDS and other diseases. In the progress chart released on the expiration of the MDGs in 2015, whereas Oceania demonstrated poor progress or deterioration in respect of five of the goals, North Africa exhibited poor progress or deterioration against only two.[11] Oceania was shown to be on target or to have made excellent progress in respect of just one MDG, compared with seven in North Africa.

The performance of the Pacific in respect of the MDGs points to a deeply troubling future if nothing is done to change the trajectory of development in the region. On current trends, by the end of this decade, it will be the poorest region in the world, with the worst maternal and infant mortality rates, the worst education outcomes, and the shortest life expectancy.

Sprent Dabwido was the president of Nauru from November 2011 to June 2013. I first met him in 2012, when he was thirty-nine years old. Like all Nauruans, he had distinct Australian sensibilities. Sprent liked his Australian beer, and he even spoke with just a hint of Aussie twang, like his countrymen and women. Although a fan of St Kilda in the Australian Football League, he told me he had a soft spot for the Cats—five years my junior, Sprent had attended Geelong Grammar School just a few years after me. It also became clear, as Sprent and I spoke, that he had not been well. He was suffering from serious health issues that had started to take their toll. He was talking and acting like he was approaching the last years of his life. In deep denial of being anywhere near middle age myself, yet still older than Sprent, this was shocking to me.

Sprent Dabwido died on 8 May 2019. He was forty-six, a dreadfully early end. And yet in Nauru, the average life expectancy for men is fifty-seven years—in Australia, it's eighty-one. Sprent's tragedy is, for Nauruans, relatively normal, and that makes it a tragedy of enormous scale.

I often think about Sprent. In many ways we had much in common. We had gone to the same privileged school. We had both chosen public service as our vocation. And yet we found ourselves, a few decades later, at radically different places along life's journey: me in the middle, him rapidly approaching the end. And this difference was only explicable in terms of the fortune of birthplace.

The Pacific's performance against the MDGs and its development challenges have a great deal to do with Australia. The failure of our strategic policy in the region is a big part of this miserable picture. The Pacific's sad development story is the single clearest reason for why Australia must transform its relationship with our island neighbours. We have the capacity, and the duty, to change their future.

STRUGGLES OVER DEMOCRACY

As the nations of the Pacific sought independence, they made efforts to introduce democracy as the form of governance throughout the region. To the enormous credit of the departing colonial authorities, these were successful. But at the same time, in general, this was done without any real empathy regarding the complex societies and cultural norms of the island nations. Crucially, the importance of reciprocity in many Pacific cultures was simply not considered. The failure to appreciate the intricacies of local life served to amplify deeply rooted divisions that had often been perpetuated by colonialism.

Asking for a vote feels a lot like asking for a favour. So what would the principle of reciprocity demand be given in return? Would it be enough to refer to a platform that one would implement if elected? Or would a more immediate and tangible offering be required, such as the payment of money? The Pacific is coloured with tribes and groups with strong cultural identities. Could democracy overcome these dividing lines? Would the outcomes of elections be accepted?

As the colonial authorities, including Australia, granted independence, these questions were neither asked nor answered. Instead, it was assumed that

the Westminster system would suffice. We over-
looked the fact that this system is itself full of cultural
nuances that have been attuned to Anglo-Celtic
culture over hundreds of years. We forgot that this
system of democracy is itself an imperfect one. To be
sure, there is genius in the Westminster system, and it
has worked in many ways in the Pacific. But along the
journey, corruption has taken hold to varying degrees
in various countries, and this presents a serious
challenge to the future prosperity of the region.

Perhaps the best example of adapting the
Westminster system to accord to cultural norms is
Samoa. There, the role of elders (*matai*) in the community, and the way in which reciprocity should be
interpreted in the context of an election campaign
(*o'o* or *momoli*), are built into Samoan democracy.
Only a *matai*, with their elevated status within an
extended family group, is eligible to stand for election.
The Samoan system has been criticised for how this
qualification to stand for election undermines the
democratic process by limiting the field of candidates
to only a few. Yet men and women become *matais*
through a complicated process which requires them

to have standing within their community. This is not very different to the experience a viable candidate for Australia's parliament would need. In fact, in many respects, it is no more or less democratic than the House of Lords. The result is that the Samoan Parliament has a status within that society which makes cultural sense.

When candidates stand for parliament, they are allowed to practice *o'o* within a set period prior to an election. This means that, in asking people for their vote, they are able to show reciprocity through the holding of a feast or some other offering. Whereas in other countries the practice of vote buying can stem from the cultural ethic of reciprocity, in Samoa it is acknowledged and built into the system. As such, the relatively new concept of democracy has been reconciled with cultural norms that have existed for millennia. It is no coincidence that Samoa is the country that suffers the least from the scourge of corruption across the Pacific.

Australia has been quick to judge the Pacific for the extent of corruption within it. At the same time, there has been little willingness on our part to try to understand its causes and to help alleviate its consequences. To assume that we are better people than those of the Pacific because we don't suffer from corruption in the same way is, to put it simply, not right.

Corruption in the region is certainly an issue. But Australia has played a part in its creation. It is time we tried to come to grips with the phenomenon and, both meaningfully and sensitively, accelerate its remediation.

Democracy is not an outlier in the Pacific, but we cannot take the future of democracy in the region for granted. We need to be just as vigilant about human rights there as we are about human rights in any other part of the world. There have been flirtations with autocratic rule in the Pacific, and as in all democracies, there is difference and division. To that end, it is essential that civilian control of the armed forces is a non-negotiable standard of local governance, as are an independent judiciary, a free media and accountable policing.

Australia has a key role to play in supporting Pacific nations as they work towards these norms.

SURVIVAL AT STAKE

Kiribati, with its far-flung atolls, is the only country that straddles all four hemispheres of the globe. The highest point across its inhabited islands is only a few metres above sea level. Yet, as confronting as rising sea levels are, the current challenge presented by climate change is a lack of water—ironic, given the ocean is already lapping some local homes.

In each Kiribati village, there is a *maneaba* (meeting house). These ingeniously designed structures have high thatched roofs with edges that come down to about 1.5 metres off the ground. Large wooden poles made from coconut trees form the supporting structure. The floors are often concrete slabs nowadays, but traditionally they were sandy soil. The massive roof provides maximum shelter from the tropical sun while retaining the cooling effects of the sea breezes. On a searing hot day in these atolls, entering a *maneaba* and sitting on the floor is the only way to get some respite from the stifling heat.

The *maneaba* is where the villagers gather. It is also the place where a traditional welcome to country is performed for visitors. I have witnessed this at the Eita *maneaba*, one of the oldest in the nation. Here, in the centre of the Kiribati capital, South Tarawa, visiting dignitaries take a sip of coconut juice while sitting cross-legged in a circle. The key leaders in the village each make a speech of welcome, and the honoured guests give a reply. It is a ritual that has existed for millennia, one I was fortunate to observe during visits to Kiribati by UN secretary-general Ban Ki-moon and governor-general Quentin Bryce, among others.

I once asked one of the local elders about the significance of this practice. I was told that the ritual we had just experienced was actually not that old. Traditionally, a cup of water drawn from the village well would have been passed around the circle—an offering of water, as the most precious Kiribati commodity, was believed to be the most momentous way to welcome a visitor. But in recent years, the well at Eita had become undrinkable due to salinisation. While this was in part a function of the overcrowding on South Tarawa, it also related to climate change.

Whenever a severe storm hit the atoll, salt water contaminated the natural fresh water underneath the coral. In the months after such a weather event, the water lens—the lighter layer of groundwater floating above the sea water—had the ability to flush itself out and return to being drinkable. However, an increased frequency of storms over South Tarawa had meant the water could no longer refresh itself and was now permanently salty. As a result, coconut juice has become the proxy drink.

In fact, more than half of the once fresh water across South Tarawa is now contaminated and unusable. Only two-thirds of the country's population have access to clean water, and only 40 per cent of people get proper sanitation.[12] This has profoundly impacted life on the most populous atoll in Kiribati, including changing a deeply significant cultural ritual practised here for thousands of years.

The coral-atoll nations of Kiribati, Tuvalu and the Marshall Islands are on the front line of climate change, each wrestling with the very survival of their island homes. The scale of this disaster is hard for us to comprehend, but fully grasp it we must.

THE CHALLENGES OF THE ISLAND STATE

Of all the challenges faced by the Pacific nations, the reality of small populations that are geographically remote is arguably the greatest.

Growing an economy is not an easy thing in itself, but as acknowledged in the Australian Government's '2017 Foreign Policy White Paper', Pacific nations face the added difficulty of building a viable economy with a small population.[13] Their economies are highly concentrated on a few activities, rather than being naturally hedged in the way that larger, more diverse economies are—a drop in tourism or the price of fish cannot be offset by other industries. Also, the cost of sending products to market is enormous, as is the cost of importing goods and services.

For a number of the countries, their largest economic asset is their exclusive economic zone (EEZ), which in some cases is vast. However, exploiting the opportunity this represents is challenging. How can a country like Tuvalu, with a population of just over 11 000, possibly manage a piece of real estate half the size of Queensland?

I remember visiting Tuvalu in 2011 and seeing an intercepted illegal fishing vessel sitting in Funafuti lagoon. I asked my host what would happen next. This was the dilemma: the vessel had been abandoned, but there was no prospect of prosecuting the owner through the Tuvaluan court system, let alone enforcing any judgment, because Tuvalu is simply not big enough to have that kind of legal infrastructure.

On the face of it, Papua New Guinea, with its population of 8.6 million people, appears to be the exception when it comes to delivering infrastructure and basic government functions. There are parts of Port Moresby that look and feel like a modern city, with hotels, shopping malls and cinemas. In many ways, though, the challenges of being small and remote also apply to that country; for example, only 23 per cent of Papua New Guineans have access to electricity. The nation is really a collection of tiny, isolated communities—such as those I encountered in Madang Province in 1984—which experience issues similar to those of a small island state. When you get a glimpse of the real Port Moresby, or the country's parliament, you begin to notice a distinctiveness which reminds you that this is a nation of twenty-two culturally and physically separate provinces.

To overcome the challenge of delivering government services, small island states around the world have engaged in a high degree of cooperative governance. A state-run university, for example, is a relatively sophisticated and complex government service. In the Pacific, countries have worked together to provide tertiary education through the University of the South Pacific (USP). It's a multinational public institution that has its administration and largest campus in Suva, Fiji and its law faculty in Port Vila, Vanuatu—the model is not unique, bearing a striking resemblance to the University of the West Indies in the Caribbean. The USP is overseen by the Council of Regional Organisations of the Pacific, which is itself under the auspices of the Pacific Island Forum (PIF). The PIF is the region's premier political and economic policy organisation, founded in 1971 with the objective of working towards peace, harmony, security, social inclusion and prosperity, so that all Pacific people can lead free, healthy and productive lives. (At the time of writing, the PIF's unity was being threatened by a serious dispute—it's incumbent on the Australian Government to do everything it can to resolve this.) Collectively, these organisations cover areas of governance ranging from fisheries control to policing to environmental management. Each is an example of the sharing of sovereignty that is an intrinsic part of the small island state story.

The sharing of sovereignty in the Pacific also occurs with large neighbours. Mail services throughout the four states of Micronesia—Yap, Chuuk, Pohnpei, and Kosrae—are provided by the US Postal Service. In Niue and the Cook Islands, a range of health and education services are provided by New Zealand. Both of these examples have occurred within the framework of longstanding government-to-government agreements between the small island states on the one hand and their larger partners on the other. These agreements not only share government service delivery, they also challenge simplistic binary notions of sovereignty.

The '2017 Foreign Policy White Paper' identifies facilitation of access for Tonga, Tuvalu and Nauru to Australian pharmaceutical testing services to improve the quality and reliability of their medicines. This is a sound first step, but we should not stop there. There is enormous scope for changing the development realities of the Pacific through greater and more effective sharing of government service delivery. Ultimately, this is the best way of countering the dilemma of an ocean of small, remote communities.

Of course, while the story of the Pacific is uniquely accented, it is fundamentally a narrative that is common to all small island states. As the campaign for Australia's election to the United Nations Security Council proceeded through the course of 2011 and 2012, I had the unique opportunity to visit most of the world's small island states. I found that the saga of small populations trying to build viable economies in the middle of oceans kept repeating itself. Industries such as tourism and fisheries kept coming to the fore. There was a common difficulty in developing an affordable energy supply when diesel power generation was the staple and the cost of transporting the diesel in the first place added a substantial premium to the cost of electricity. Economics drove renewable energy uptake, and sovereignty and sharing arrangements followed.

It also became clear to me that Australia's understanding of the small island state context is unique among the developed nations. Except for New Zealand, no other such nation has a similarly engaged relationship with a group of small island states such as Australia has with the Pacific. And in this regard, our reputation has preceded us.

The Caribbean knows us through the Commonwealth and cricket. But the region also knows that, because of our history in the Pacific, we understand its strategic circumstances. Moreover, it has been keen for us to be the bridge between it and the Pacific. The archipelagic Seychelles in the Indian Ocean likewise desperately wants Australia to look west and show more interest in it, because it knows that we intrinsically understand so much of what it faces.

The Alliance of Small Island States (AOSIS) has forty-four members, making it the second-largest grouping in the United Nations behind Africa, which has fifty-five members. With little additional effort, Australia's expertise in the Pacific affords us the opportunity to become the partner of choice among developed countries across the entirety of

AOSIS. For a nation like Australia, which is not part of any geopolitically organised grouping, such as the European Union or the African Union, this opportunity is priceless.

And yet, right now, it is a prospect that is being ignored.

AUSTRALIA'S CONTEMPORARY POSTURE

It would be wrong to suggest that Australia has not properly allocated resources to its relationship with the Pacific. On the contrary, we are genuinely present in the region, maintaining formal relations with all the Pacific nations and a diplomatic presence with fifteen of the seventeen other PIF members. In addition, every year, about 40 per cent of our global aid program—more than A$1 billion of development assistance—goes to the Pacific. According to the Lowy Institute, Australia accounts for 45 per cent of the total aid given to the region; by comparison, New Zealand provides around 9 per cent, China and the United States 8 per cent each, and Japan 6 per cent.[14]

Our largest Defence Cooperation Program is with Papua New Guinea, to the tune of A\$42 million. This reflects a high degree of collaboration, particularly through officer training between the Australian Defence Force (ADF) and the PNG Defence Force (PNGDF). Similarly, over many decades, a significant amount of training has been provided to the Republic of Fiji Military Force by the ADF, while the Tonga Defence Services also enjoys its closest military relationship with the ADF. And every year, officers from international defence forces graduate from the Royal Military College, Duntroon. This is critically important defence diplomacy. The trials and tribulations of officer training forge a bond between officers that last a lifetime. Since 2010, 126 PNG officers have graduated, thirty-seven from Fiji and twelve from Tonga, strengthening a unique link between our army and the defence forces of the Pacific.

The Pacific Patrol Boat Program provides patrol boats to every nation in the PIF (excluding New Zealand). For each of the three Pacific countries which maintain a military—Papua New Guinea, Fiji and Tonga—these patrol boats constitute their entire navy; in each of the other countries, the boats are highly prized and play a significant role in the policing of their vast EEZs. With each vessel, the Royal Australian Navy provides in-country advisory personnel, maintenance support, crew training and technical assistance. Even in the two PIF countries where we do not have a formal diplomatic presence—the Marshall Islands and Tokelau—there are still Australian Government representatives on the ground fulfilling an effective and essential diplomatic role.

But while Australia clearly has committed substantial resources to the Pacific, something is lacking: intent. The sense of purpose around how these resources should be used and to what end has been weak. 'Why has Australia been devoting resources to the Pacific?' is a question rarely asked, and when it has been raised, poorly answered. What we are left with is policy drift.

Over the years, we have had plenty of strategies dedicated to clarifying Australia's role in East Asia, in the countries of the Association of Southeast Asian Nations, even in the Middle East. For the Department of Foreign Affairs and Trade (DFAT) and the

Department of Defence, the key bilateral relationships are appropriately with the United States and China. Significant emphasis is also placed upon countries in Europe. Again, this is all fair enough. But at the same time, strategic thinking about the Pacific has been non-existent.

Major diplomatic postings in DFAT, such as to the United States, China, Indonesia and Great Britain, have all been done at the deputy secretary level. And yet the most senior person looking after the entirety of the Pacific has been a first assistant secretary, the level below.

The bias against the Pacific is evident right at the start of the foreign affairs adventure. Young graduate entrants into our diplomatic corps look longingly at a first posting to New York or Geneva. For those who end up in Honiara or Nuku'alofa, there is a sense of having drawn the short straw. And with that, the view about the relative insignificance of the Pacific becomes institutionalised.

Increasingly, successful diplomatic careers are being built on a specialisation—China, multilateralism, South-East Asia. Pacific experience, however, is still regarded as part of a diplomat's generalist toolkit. Navigating the complexities of the region requires as much sophistication and nuance as any other in which we conduct foreign policy. It therefore needs to be a respected and desirable speciality within our diplomatic corps.

This lack of interest in the Pacific is not limited to DFAT. Wander through the corridors of Parliament House and you'll find no shortage of advisers who will offer a view on Israel and Palestine. Yet since Papua New Guinea's independence in 1975, how many members of successive cabinets could have provided a serious opinion about the state of the Pacific?

The truth is that serious mainstream policy intent concerning the Pacific, within any part of the Australian Government, has been missing in action for a long time. Some of the most senior and accomplished members of our public service have served there, yet consecutive governments and the bureaucracy have not made the most of their expertise. Serious thinking about the region has been left to a small but very dedicated group within DFAT and Defence who are incredibly well informed and have knowledge of global significance. But while there are a number of people around the globe interested in hearing their voices, this has not, until very recently, been the case in Canberra.

As another example, our universities, particularly the Australian National University's College of Asia and the Pacific, which includes the Pacific Institute, focus on the region more than any other academics in the world do. Yet this still attracts far fewer academic resources than it did forty years ago. In a different context, non-government organisations such as Care, World Vision and Oxfam all report the comparative difficulty of raising money for disaster relief in the Pacific relative to similar campaigns centred on Africa. The emotional pull of one cause far exceeds that of the other, even though the Pacific is our neighbourhood.

In these differing ways, interest in the Pacific within Australian society is scant. Since Papua New Guinea achieved independence, when there were five times as many Australians living there as now, our knowledge about the region has shrunk. And somewhere along the way, Australians stopped caring.

This must change. And it is government that has to lead a national revival of Pacific interest.

There has always been a belief in government that Australia has obligations, but the tendency has been to tick boxes rather than solve problems. Whenever an Australian Government representative provides a Pacific report card, it's invariably couched in terms of actions, detailing our projects, interactions, expenditure. But very rarely does it explain how a specific problem is being solved. Almost never will there be a report about the diminishment of a disease or an improvement in educational outcomes or the betterment of living standards. Only the inputs are reported, not the outcomes.

This is in part because an outcome-based report, such as that on the MDGs, would make depressing reading. But it is also because of the obligation-centric way in which we have framed our Pacific engagement. It is as if the primary concern is whether we have met our obligations—the changing of Pacific realities comes a distant second.

Accordingly, the Pacific has been subjected to holding-pattern policies by Australian governments.

Immediate crises are managed, while the fundamental dilemmas of island life remain largely unchanged and the development gap continues to grow. What is missing is policy based on a determined decision that, as a nation, we care about the Pacific's development, and we mean to act in a way which will transform its trajectory. Our obligations are important, but it is the future of the Pacific peoples themselves that must be the catalyst for our actions.

The '2017 Foreign Policy White Paper' mentioned earlier in this book is the most recent comprehensive statement of Australian foreign policy. Chapter seven, titled 'A shared agenda for security and prosperity', surveys the existing Australian presence and programs in the Pacific. Taken as a list, it looks significant— and in some ways, it is. Yet there is very little that is new, that takes Australia's agenda forward.

The White Paper talks impressively about Australia's 'commitment to work with governments in the Pacific to respond to climate change' and to improve health 'outcomes'.[15] Yet the Morrison government, which inherited these aims from the Turnbull government that oversaw the crafting of the White

Paper, has patently failed the Pacific on the question of climate change. And Australia's development assistance has drifted away from supporting health outcomes. While the talk is strong, the walk is weak.

In fact, the fundamental rationale for our interest in the Pacific, as expressed in the White Paper, is breathtakingly brief. There is a reference to 'common interests' and the importance of stability in Papua New Guinea and the broader Pacific in order 'to defend Australia's northern approaches, secure our borders and protect our exclusive economic zone'.[16] But this is a long way from understanding that our actions play a defining role in the way Australia relates to the world. If our efforts in the Pacific are to succeed, then our motivations must be centred not only on our own fortunes but also on those of the people of the Pacific.

The clearest indication of the Pacific's low priority in the White Paper is where it has been placed in the document's overall structure. The Pacific chapter is the second-last. Chapters one and two deal with where Australia sits in the world and contain appropriate and frequent references to the United States, China, Europe and India. At the same time, Morocco,

Syria, North Korea and Nigeria all rate a mention. By contrast, there are only two specific yet passing references to the Pacific, and not one of its island states is mentioned by name.

In early 2018, the Coalition government's interest in the Pacific spiked, largely inspired, it seemed, by a series of reports in the Fairfax media about the prospect of a Chinese military base being built in Vanuatu. These reports were denied by the governments of both China and Vanuatu. Although there is something deeply misguided about this sudden interest in the Pacific because of the purported actions of another country there, given the absence of interest otherwise, we should welcome the fact that the region is finally on the radar of the current government. Nonetheless, it is now time for a genuine transformation in Australia's posture towards the Pacific.

FORMIDABLE EXPERTISE

Our significant presence in the Pacific has allowed us to acquire formidable regional expertise. However, this wisdom is not yet properly valued.

Having spent seventeen months solely focused on the Pacific, in March 2012, in addition to being the parliamentary secretary for Pacific island affairs, I was appointed the parliamentary secretary for foreign affairs. This saw me play a more global role, particularly in the lead-up to the vote which would see Australia elected to the UN Security Council. As I spent more time talking to diplomats about our bilateral relationships beyond the Pacific, I was struck by how frequently, at the end of a conversation, the topic would turn to our region.

Representatives of European countries were invariably interested in the efforts of other developed nations to engage in development assistance. While they would naturally focus on development in Africa, they sought my view about progress in the Pacific. There was deep acknowledgement of Australia's expertise in the region. In regards to Africa, the perspective was different but the interest just as great. Many countries on that continent were struggling with their own development challenges and saw in the Pacific another part of the world experiencing a similar journey. Questions about health and education challenges abounded. African nations also expected us to take a leading role in the Pacific.

Australia's deep understanding of the Pacific is also clearly recognised by the United States. In 2011, I remember talking with a senior American official about this subject. There was a certain frustration on his part. He appreciated the views being shared about many parts of the world, particularly Asia, but his attempts to seek a direction from Australia concerning policy intent in the Pacific had come to nought. The United States is a global superpower, he assured me. It had assets and resources and influence, he continued, adding that the United States was willing to place them at our disposal in the Pacific if we would only tell them what we wanted them to do.

This conversation was a revelation to me. As I tried to defend Australia's honour, the truth was that I utterly shared his frustration. I was a relatively junior figure trying to assert my opinions and ideas, but I was constantly coming up against an entrenched view of the world which had the Pacific a long way from the centre of Australia's perceived national interest.

The United States is the subject of our most important bilateral relationship. This association is wide and deep, covering everything from defence to sport to medical research. Inevitably, it is a relationship characterised by Australia following America's lead. This makes sense: the United States has a population of nearly 330 million, is the world's largest economy, and is a true superpower, whereas Australia has a population of 25 million people, is the fourteenth-largest economy globally, and is a middle power. In other words, they are big and we are not. And yet there is one area where the United States invariably looks to Australia to take the lead: the Pacific. It is the space in our relationship where we have the opportunity to demonstrate how we behave as leaders, making it a crucial part of that relationship.

This argument about the significance of the Pacific holds true in respect of all our global relationships. But in this context, Australia's reluctance to lead has left the United States with a sense of bewilderment.

It is simply essential that Australia demonstrates leadership in the Pacific. This is first and foremost for the region's sake, but a close secondary benefit is that it presents an opportunity to amplify and frame the mutuality of our US alliance. While we are not equals with the United States, the obligations we have to each other are two-way. The Pacific proves it. And if, through the Pacific, we are able to better assert this mutuality, it will build the leadership side of Australia's international personality.

Whether we like it or not, in a very significant way, the Pacific is our global calling card. While our expertise there is globally acknowledged, we are also defined by our actions there. For now, that assessment is largely positive. In a region where North America and Europe play a lesser role, our efforts are valued. But if the Pacific continues on its current trajectory and becomes the least developed part of the world, this judgement will change. Questions will naturally be asked, such as: 'What was Australia doing?' And it will have happened on our watch. Australia's actions in the next few years must radically change to ensure that the overall quality of life in the Pacific begins to improve, and that such questions never have to get asked.

THE QUESTION OF AUSTRALIAN LEADERSHIP

Australia is a friendly, capable, well-resourced and trusted country. As a result, we are easy to work with. People around the world like us, a lot. Indeed, we might be the best diplomats in the world. The over-whelming success of Australia's bid to win a seat on the UN Security Council in 2012 is testament to this. It was a boon for our strategic circumstances.

And we are most comfortable working in a team—with another country as captain. Until World War II, the captain of most of the teams to which we belonged was Great Britain. Since then, it has largely been the United States. This dynamic describes Australia's major military engagements, from the Boer War at the end of the nineteenth century, through both world wars and Vietnam in the twentieth century, and in the Middle East this century.

There are some examples of international leader-ship in Australia's recent history. Gareth Evans as foreign affairs minister played a pivotal role in creatively shepherding Cambodia out of the Khmer Rouge period and the Vietnamese occupation—modern

Cambodia owes much to his efforts. Under the Howard government, Australia played a crucial role in ending the Bougainville conflict. The agreement that provided for the recent referendum in that PNG province, and which is guiding the shape of Bougainville's relationship with Port Moresby, was brokered by Australia. And it was Australia that in 2003 put together the Regional Assistance Mission to Solomon Islands (RAMSI), widely regarded as global best practice in terms of an intervention resulting in an end to conflict and a transition to a peaceful and functional society.

These initiatives prove that when we try, Australia can lead, and do it well. They put the betterment of people in our broader region first, which in turn served Australia's national interest. And yet, when considered within the broad sweep of Australia's post-Federation strategic policy, these are the exceptions which prove the rule.

Historically, our involvement in the Pacific has been focused on delivering development assistance through overseas aid. This has largely been put to good use—it has made a difference. But the emphasis on aid alone has limited our imagination when it comes to how Australia engages and cooperates with the Pacific. When asked to do more in our international neighbourhood, we reflexively spend even more and facilitate more trips. Yet while aid and face-to-face meetings are important, on their own they do not constitute a plan of action for Australia in the Pacific.

Defining our contribution to the region in terms of infrastructure projects is not playing to our strengths. There are many countries with bigger economies than us that can make far greater contributions to large projects. This is an arena in which we will quickly become a secondary player. When it comes to the spreading of largesse through state visits, Australia also plays in the junior league.

The way we have acted in the past will not help us to build our strategic weight in the Pacific in the future. Australia's plan needs to be bigger in its scope and smarter in its conception. In fact, there are many ways open to us beyond development assistance to impact the fortunes of the Pacific. Providing access to our economy, and to our government's service delivery, for example, offer much bigger opportunities for positive change than a simple focus on aid. Our biggest strength in the region is the natural affinity which the local peoples have with Australia, and commonalities in language, law, government structures and even sport give us an unrivalled head start over other nations.

New Zealand is, of course, central to our strategy in the Pacific. Sometimes Australia suffers from an inferiority complex when it comes to those across the Tasman. We have a tendency to believe that the true leader in the Pacific, the country with greater regional expertise than our own, is New Zealand. Certainly, New Zealand identifies closely with the Pacific—the Māori are Polynesian, and Auckland has a Pacific character unlike that of any city in Australia. But still, this view is erroneous.

Australia has a presence and a history which gives us an understanding of the Pacific that is every bit as informed and detailed as that of New Zealand, if not more so when it comes to areas such as Melanesia and Micronesia. It is just that New Zealand gives the Pacific greater value in its world view and has a clearer sense of purpose regarding its actions here. Fortunately, this means that our respective roles in the Pacific are entirely complementary. There is much that Australia can learn from New Zealand about the Pacific, especially how to engage with purpose. And there is great capability that we can add to New Zealand's efforts, as long as we're willing to work much more closely with our Kiwi neighbours.

A SUBSTANTIVE AGENDA

Climate Change

Unlocking all forms of engagement in the Pacific requires one critical key: Australia must have a credible position around action on climate change. While this has been a strength in the past, it is a key failure right now.

In July 2011, Marcus Stephen, who was in his final year as the president of Nauru, participated in the first ever debate of the UN Security Council about the security implications of climate change. Around that time, he wrote an opinion piece published in *The New York Times* in which he said that climate change 'threatens the very existence of many countries in the Pacific … Already, Nauru's coast, the only habitable area, is steadily eroding … The low-lying nations of Tuvalu, Kiribati and the Marshall Islands may vanish entirely within our grandchildren's lifetimes'.[17] These realities for the Pacific are profound and confronting. President Stephen addressed the Security Council in person because the Pacific, more than anywhere else in the world, is on the front line of climate change, the effects of which are many and manifest.

In 2005, the communities living on the Carteret Islands of Papua New Guinea made the heart-wrenching decision to try to leave their homes and move to the main island of Bougainville. Bigger tides and more frequent storms were seeing houses and vegetable gardens washed away. The basics of life—food, water and shelter—were all becoming more difficult to secure in the Carterets. The obvious consequence of the move—severe dislocation for these communities—had become the lesser of two evils.

Such a move, however, is not simple. Significant land is required on Bougainville, almost all of which is occupied by the traditional owners. As of 2018,

81 hectares had been secured from the Catholic Church, which owns four abandoned plantations. Using this, just fourteen family parcels had been developed for the Carteret Islanders. Where to move the vast bulk of the islanders is an issue that remains unresolved.

This can be regarded as one of the first examples of climate change–induced migration in the world. The societal tensions and sundry other difficulties which arise from it are plain to see.

Of all the effects of climate change, the one which gives rise to the greatest fight for survival is water security, a vulnerability that was brought into sharp relief during the Tuvalu drought of 2011. In October of that year, this small coral atoll nation, which lies a few hundred kilometres north of Fiji, was gripped by an unprecedented dry. The main atoll of Funafuti was down to just a few days' worth of water supply, its inhabitants subsisting on only two buckets of water per day.

When I heard about the crisis, I was surprised. I had been in Funafuti just a few months earlier and there had been no talk of water shortages. But

Funafuti, unlike other atolls, has no water lens to provide drinking water. Rather, tanks set up around people's homes collect rainwater, tanks that are big enough to hold a six-week supply. So the reason no-one on the atoll had flagged a water shortage when I'd been there was that, in the everyday context, there was no shortage. However, the water security of Funafuti is based on minimal infrastructure in the context of a highly predictable rain pattern. When changes in the climate altered that pattern just a little, the country experienced a sudden water crisis. Both Australia and New Zealand responded by providing Tuvalu with a portable desalination plant. Nonetheless, this drought brought home to me a great vulnerability of the region.

There is no bigger issue in the Pacific than climate change. And for Australia to engage meaningfully with the island states, we must come to terms with climate change ourselves. But the current government has failed to do this, and the fallout from this was most obvious at the 2019 PIF in Tuvalu.

The forum's Smaller Island States grouping had formulated a declaration on climate change which they proposed as the main outcome of the gathering. But Australia, represented by Prime Minister Morrison, stood in the way of its adoption, which put us squarely at odds with the region. The effect this had on Australia's relationship with the Pacific was summed up by the forum's host, then Tuvalu prime minister Enele Sopoaga, who said that he had been 'stunned' by Morrison's approach. He went on to say: 'That was the tone of the discussion. Please don't expect that we come and bow down … we were exchanging flaring language—not swearing—but of course expressing the concerns of leaders'.[18]

It was also clear that the negative sentiments towards Australia had damaged the Pacific bond well beyond concerns about climate change. Sopoaga said the encounter made him recollect meetings past where 'colonial masters' had called the shots. He said: 'We are still seeing reflections and manifestations of this neocolonialist approach to what the leaders are talking about'.

These words are unambiguous: if Australia gets this issue wrong, it will jeopardise our relationship with all of the Pacific. The Pacific wants Australia to have a credible policy to reduce our own emissions. And it wants Australia to support the Pacific in telling its climate-change story to the world.

I was sitting next to president Stephen when he addressed the UN Security Council in New York back in 2011. After he spoke, I delivered a speech on behalf of Australia that supported what he had said. Soon after, the Gillard government facilitated a visit by Ban Ki-moon to the Solomon Islands and Kiribati, and I was fortunate enough to accompany the secretary-general. We stood together in one family's kitchen in Tarawa, where at high tide the water lapped through the door. We planted mangroves at the water's edge with then Kiribati president Anote Tong, to help establish a natural seawall during storms. That trip exemplified the role Australia can play in helping the Pacific to change the rest of the world's response to climate change.

Fast-forward a decade from this constructive and diplomatic effort, and any meaningful action on climate change has completely stalled due to the tribal ideology of the current Coalition government. Not only has Morrison utterly failed to deliver a coherent emissions-reduction strategy for Australia, we rank last on the 2020 Climate Change Performance Index. And, as the 2019 PIF made clear, the Morrison government has no interest in assisting the Pacific to tell its story to the world.

Cooperation on Defence

A fundamental way of improving both the security and the prosperity of the Pacific is by maximising our defence cooperation.

Between 1998 and 2003, the Solomon Islands experienced The Tensions—over those five years, a period characterised by violence and corruption, the nation suffered a major breakdown in its governance, economy and law and order. In July 2003, after a request from the Solomons Government, Operation Helpem Fren—RAMSI—was launched to restore peace to the island state. This was a mission led by a significant military effort but which also included policing and support for government administration. Over the next fourteen years, thousands of defence, police and civilian personnel from fifteen participating countries around the Pacific rebuilt the order and institutions of the Solomons Government.

RAMSI was a triumph in regional cooperation. It was a model for how an international intervention supported by a local community can restore peace in a nation—indeed, after a decade of RAMSI, 86 per cent of Solomon Islanders were supportive of the work of the mission.[19] It was also a powerful example of how Australian defence cooperation with the Pacific can dramatically improve the region's security environment. RAMSI, which was led by Australia, directed significant goodwill towards us, not only from the Solomons but also from the other participating nations. I had the honour of visiting the RAMSI headquarters in the Solomons capital Honiara numerous times, and I felt a sense of great pride while witnessing both Ban Ki-moon and Quentin Bryce's reactions to Australia's role in the endeavour. National security is at the centre of any nation's core interests. And through RAMSI, the Pacific wholeheartedly welcomed Australia's defence engagement.

The extent of our defence cooperation in the Pacific is already substantial. The Defence Cooperation

Program with Papua New Guinea is the largest of these initiatives. It involves thirty-five members of the ADF being based in that country, and there would hardly be an officer in the PNGDF who has not undertaken a defence course at some stage in Australia. A number of joint exercises are held between the ADF and the PNGDF, most notably the annual maritime Exercise Paradise, as well as Exercise Olgeta Warrior, which has been taking place regularly for over a decade. The joint initiative at Lombrum Naval Base on Manus Island is another significant development.

Similarly, longstanding relationships with the Republic of Fiji Military Forces and the Tonga Defence Services have seen Australia provide a great deal of training to the local leadership.

Taken together, this all represents a major commitment to the region through the ADF. But more can be done.

For many of these countries, participating in UN missions is a significant means by which their defence forces experience active deployment. There is a role for Australia in providing training to assist these personnel in becoming ready to perform such missions.

The militaries of Papua New Guinea, Fiji and Tonga are small and have understandable capability gaps. For example, despite aviation being a central remedy to the logistical challenge of life in the Pacific, there is very little in the way of airforces in the region. Just as Australia has been able to fill the capability gap of local naval power through the Pacific Patrol Boat Program, a forensic look at aerial capacity will create opportunities for Australia to help Pacific militaries to improve their air defence abilities. These efforts would clearly be in Australia's national interest, and—compared with the cost of our current international deployments—they would be cheap.

A greater program of exercises with the militaries of the region could be done in concert with New Zealand, the United States and France. In turn, Australia should work with New Zealand to look at how both countries can maximise the interoperability of their defence forces within the Pacific.

A more militarily capable Pacific helps build sovereignty for the region's nations and greater independence in their decision-making. Australia can play a unique role in supporting this aspiration.

Accessing the Australian Economy

In 2008, the Gillard government announced the Pacific Seasonal Worker Pilot Scheme. Based on a similar arrangement established in New Zealand, it allowed workers from a list of Pacific countries to come to Australia and work in the horticulture industry for six months at a time. The scheme was developed in concert with both the horticulture industry and the trade union movement. It provided for Australian award conditions of employment, and it operated in a sector with a highly transient labour force.

For the industry, the scheme offered the prospect of a consistent workforce from one season to the next. It saved growers from having to train the workers from scratch before every harvest and accordingly yielded significant productivity gains. It also meant moving away from an undocumented workforce and all the risks that came with this.

For the Australian labour movement, the scheme meant that the industry could be better brought into the mainstream labour market, under explicit terms and conditions of employment. In turn, this reduced exploitation in the workforce, which is at the heart of the labour movement's mission.

For many Pacific workers, the scheme transformed their lives. They were given the opportunity to earn Australian wages and remit them home. Better homes were then being built, local business opportunities were being pursued with real money behind them, and health and education more generally were being improved.

In 2012, the Pacific Seasonal Worker Pilot Scheme was renamed the Seasonal Worker Program and expanded to include work in the pastoral, aquaculture, cane, cotton and accommodation sectors. The true impact of this unambiguously good scheme can be seen in the numbers. From 2012 through June 2020, 47 802 visas were granted to people participating in the scheme.[20] The World Bank estimates that the net gains for the countries involved from 2012–13 to 2016–17 was A$143.8 million, the majority of which made its way to the workers' homes.[21]

In Tonga's case, this amounted to A$99.4 million flowing there from the Australian economy, which equates to more than half the development assistance

Australia provided to Tonga over the same period (A$184.9 million).[22] The impact on Tonga has been huge and overwhelmingly positive. But Australia has also benefited greatly because during that half-decade, Tongan workers also contributed to our economy. This scheme demonstrates the power of the Australian economy within our broader region.

The COVID-19 pandemic has obviously interrupted Australia's efforts to open up its economy to the Pacific. However, as soon as it is safe to do so, Australia must make every effort to restore the Seasonal Worker Program, ensuring that the jobs being generated are subject to Australian conditions of employment and are not exploitative. Developing an ambitious agenda for access by Pacific nations to the Australian economy is central to the successful future of Australia–Pacific engagement.

Development Assistance

In recent years, Australia's development assistance in the Pacific has stagnated. From 2007 to 2013, such aid grew from A$873 million to A$1.1 billion:

a 34 per cent increase. Yet between 2013–14 and 2018–19—during the Abbott, Turnbull and Morrison governments—the aid budget decreased by nearly 10 per cent. Thankfully, this aid was increased to A$1.4 billion in the 2019–20 budget.[23]

Managed well and strategically, overseas aid can make a real difference. In 2012, Australian aid supported Papua New Guinea in removing primary school fees throughout the country via the Tuition Fee Free program. This resulted in almost a 10 per cent increase in school attendance between 2012 and 2015 (from 78.5 per cent to 88.4 per cent).[24] This is an incredibly powerful investment in Papua New Guinea's human capital.

Relative to most countries, Australia delivers its development assistance in a highly effective manner. We walk the high road in engaging in projects which have a tremendous impact in the recipient countries, but without overly focusing on the political dividend. While a plan for Australia's engagement in the Pacific must extend beyond aid, development assistance is important because of what it says to the region about our commitment to its peoples.

A Love of Sport

There are many ways in which Australia could leverage the affinity that exists between it and the Pacific in relation to sport. Australia and the island nations of the Pacific not only share a love of sport, we share a love of many of the same sports.

As I mentioned earlier, three of the biggest days of the year in Papua New Guinea involve the State of Origin matches between Queensland and New South Wales. Papua New Guineans wear their colours on their sleeves—while most show a maroon bias, a healthy swathe of blue can also be seen among fans. Indeed, the country has a long-held ambition to field its own team in the NRL. An historic lack of interest on the part of the NRL has meant that Papua New Guinea's dream has not yet eventuated, although in recent times the league's attitude appears to have changed. This is a very welcome development. In the wake of successful trial games in February 2020 and talk of a premiership match between Australian teams being played in Port Moresby, the NRL should seize the momentum to go even further.

Using northern Queensland as a base for the medium term, it would be completely possible to establish a PNG team in the NRL. Any angst at not seeing the team enough in the short term would be ameliorated by a long-term plan to transition the team's home base to Port Moresby. What would matter from the start is that the jersey of Papua New Guinea's national Rugby League side—the Kumuls—would be seen running around the NRL's stadiums. The games would also need to be broadcast into Papua New Guinea. With the right engagement strategy, the NRL could harness local passion and build a commitment to a hometown team.

Such an outcome would place Australia's bilateral relationship with Papua New Guinea on a different plane. The cost associated with such a plan would represent the best-value spend Australia could ever make in building that relationship. Accordingly, the fulfilment of Papua New Guinea's ambitions to field a team in the NRL must be viewed in terms of an Australian national imperative. We have soft-power options aplenty and we need to start seizing these opportunities now.

COVID-19

At the time of writing, the COVID-19 pandemic continues to change the Pacific and Australia's engagement with the region, as it is changing most other aspects of the world.

The virus has been ravaging Indonesia, with which Papua New Guinea shares a porous land border—the chances of containing the disease in the province of Papua are remote. There is also little hope of managing an ordered regime of social distancing in a country where close social contact is so embedded in the culture, and the existence of other diseases within the population, such as malaria, will likely give rise to significant comorbidity factors for those infected with COVID-19. PNG's health system will struggle to cope with a significant influx of COVID-19 patients—there is not enough personal protective equipment among its health workers and an insufficient quantity of ventilators. The prospect of a significant human tragedy unfolding in Papua New Guinea is a frightening one.

Even more terrifying is the fact that the remainder of the Pacific has similar health concerns and poor health infrastructure. The disease could easily devastate the entire region. Yet, again at the time of writing, there was hope that the isolation of Pacific island countries might prevent the disease from taking hold within these communities.

Regardless, for Papua New Guinea and the wider Pacific, the economic impact of COVID-19 will be profound. Access to the Australian labour market has already been seriously reduced, and with this, the remittances back home are drying up. Tourism to the region has all but stopped. Even industries such as fishing have been affected, as critical logistics supply chains are impacted by the inability of people to engage in international travel.

In light of this crisis, Australia must emphasise support for Pacific countries, particularly their health systems—health has been a long-term strength in regards to the aid we have delivered. This emergency, in so many ways, has acted as an accelerant on global trends. In turn, this has fast-tracked the need for Australia to develop and enact a comprehensive plan of engagement with the Pacific. As a result of COVID-19, the nations of the Pacific, like all other countries, are making a stark assessment of their international relationships, deciding on who they can depend. It is essential that Australia stands as the natural partner of choice for the Pacific.

THE STRATEGIC CONTEXT

The transformation of our relationship with the Pacific matters on its own terms. It also matters for what it says about the way in which Australia engages with the world.

Australia should be at the forefront of supporting the Pacific through its advocacy for action on climate change. We should be developing a substantive agenda in the Pacific by listening to and partnering with its nations, and then encouraging countries beyond the region to invest in that agenda. Were we to show this leadership, it would represent a new Australian engagement that seeks to actively shape the strategic circumstances we face.

This is an attitude which should, of course, also apply, with appropriate calibration, to our engagement with South-East Asia. While the strategic weight of Australia is not as determinative in that region as it is in the Pacific, it remains substantial. But since the role played by Gareth Evans in the birth of modern Cambodia, we have been much less impactful in that part of world. We should have been prominent in the transition of Myanmar to democracy, just as we should be prominent in South-East Asia more generally.

We also have a significant voice in East Asia. China, Japan and South Korea are three of our five largest trading partners (the others are the United States and India). These are the relationships which, in great measure, will determine Australia's future. Yet our voice in East Asia is muted when it should be clearly heard. And this begins with leadership in the Pacific.

Together, an assertive China and an unpredictable United States give rise to the most challenging set of strategic circumstances Australia has faced since World War II. While the Cold War carried with it an existential threat that does not exist today, Australia's strategy was obvious. As a Western democracy, we needed to stand with the United States in its diplomatic contest with the Soviet Union and in the process enjoy the benefits of America's extended nuclear deterrence. The world may have been a place fraught with danger during the Cold War, but Australia's choices were clear. The current environment is much thornier because the way forward is not obvious.

Under President Xi Jinping, China is seeking to reshape the global rules-based order in a way that it has never attempted to do before. In its efforts to mould the world, China is acting as all great powers do. Yet the order established in the aftermath of World War II has served Australia and the Indo-Pacific well. As we are an island trading country, for example, the UN Convention on the Law of the Sea is central to our national interest, so China's actions in places like the South China Sea are of great concern.

Undoubtedly, our ongoing relationship with China is extremely complex. At the same time, there is a question mark over the future role of the United States both in East Asia and globally. There is an understandable desire on the part of the United States for its allies to pay their way. But what if they don't? Australia spends about 2 per cent of its gross domestic product on defence, so our alliance with the

United Sates is as solid as it has ever been. But is the future of the relationships that America has with other nations in East Asia, those that form the bedrock of its presence, as clear?

At the core of our cooperation with the United States is the desire to maintain the architecture of the existing rules-based order. Precisely because Australia has a keen interest in this order, the American alliance remains crucial. Accordingly, it is undoubtedly in Australia's national interest that the United States has a significant presence in East Asia.

Australia must itself find the answers to these strategic challenges. Australian prosperity and security in the twenty-first century will turn on the extent to which we are able to build a robust political relationship with China, albeit within the context of balancing our economic relationship with our security anxieties. Having the United States by our side and fully engaged in East Asia will be vital in navigating this path. This is all achievable if Australia acts with intent in its foreign policy, rather than engaging in foreign policy drift. And this is why the Pacific matters so much.

THE PACIFIC AND ITS PEOPLE MATTER

Our actions in the Pacific denote our place in the world, where we fall on the spectrum of internationally acknowledged leadership. A proactive plan for the development of the Pacific will consolidate the authoritative side of our international personality, demonstrating that we are actively engaged in this region and in global affairs. It will make it clear to the United States that, within the context of our alliance, Australia is willing to share the burden of strategic thought, making it easier for the United States to remain connected to our part of the world.

There is much about our circumstances that is beyond our control. But we do have strategic agency, and we will accomplish very little if we do not overcome our national inclination to sit in the second row. We can begin this work in the Pacific, firstly by establishing our motivations for taking action.

These must not be centred on denying China. If Australia's renewed interest in the Pacific is interpreted by the region as an attempt to keep China at bay, then it will be seen in a very cynical light. The Pacific is, after all, well versed in the competitive diplomacy conducted over many years by China and Taiwan. It engaged with this, even received some benefit from it. But at no point was anyone in the Pacific under any illusion that this competitiveness had much to do with them. Accordingly, those years did not build, for either China or Taiwan, the kind of long-term relationships with island states that should be the end goal of our own engagement.

Basing our actions in the Pacific on an attempt to strategically deny China would be an historic mistake. Not only would this be detrimental to our regional relationships, it would be a failed course of action. Australia has no right to expect a set of exclusive relationships with Pacific nations. They are perfectly free to engage on whatever terms they choose with China or, for that matter, any other country. Disputing this would be resented, as the recent past has shown.

In January 2018, the then minister for international development and the Pacific, Senator Concetta Fierravanti-Wells, was highly critical of the development assistance cooperation that China and various countries in the Pacific had pursued, accusing China

of constructing 'roads to nowhere' and 'useless buildings'. The reaction from the Pacific was swift and
visceral. The very next day, Samoan Prime Minister
Tuilaepa Sailele said:

> The comments by the Development Minister have
> certainly surprised me, indeed, they are quite
> insulting to the leaders of Pacific Island neighbours
> … To me the comments seem to question the
> integrity, wisdom and intelligence of the leaders
> of the Pacific Islands … These kinds of comments
> can destroy the excellent relationships existing
> between Australia and the Pacific Island neighbours,
> particularly Samoa.[25]

Prime Minister Tuilaepa is a giant of Pacific
politics and a long-time friend of Australia. Such a
scathing rebuke from this eminent figure made it
clear that Senator Fierravanti-Wells' comments did
nothing to advance the cause of Australian diplomacy
in the Pacific.

An attempt to engage in a calculated denial of
China will only create a geostrategic contest that

Pacific island countries will register with bewilderment, if not mirth. And if it prompts a bidding war from all competing parties, then from their perspective, so much the better. Besides, the idea that Australia would win a bidding war with China is laughable. Equally, the idea that Pacific nations would adhere to a call from Australia to not engage with China is silly. Such follies would be damaging to our relations with all the countries concerned.

How China relates to the Pacific is the Pacific's business. Australia's prerogative is to focus on improving its own relationships with the Pacific. We must lead in the Pacific by listening, learning and respecting. If we do this, we will start to change our relationship with the region for the better. And in the process, we will begin to generate real hope that our cooperation, based on the Pacific's genuine needs and desires, can build a new prosperity.

At the centre of Australia's motivations must be the people of the Pacific, their security and prosperity. Accordingly, building a bilateral relationship with each Pacific nation, on its own terms, must be our fundamental position. Rather than worrying about

RICHARD MARLES

the prospect of foreign military bases in the region, our real call to arms must be the Pacific's performance against the MDGs, and the associated and real risk that it will become entrenched as the least developed part of the world. The fate of ten million islanders should form the heart of our engagement. Only by demonstrating to the Pacific that our true interest really is them can we can build a deeply substantive relationship of trust and partnership.

~

The summer of 2011 was marked by tragedy in our part of the world, even by the standards of Australia's disaster-prone summers. Brisbane experienced its second-worst flood in 100 years. In Toowoomba, the flood waters created an inland tsunami unlike any phenomenon previously observed, and four people tragically lost their lives. The estimated cost of the Queensland floods was more than A$2 billion, and they remained front-page news for weeks.

And then, on 22 February 2011, an earthquake struck the New Zealand city of Christchurch.

One hundred and eighty-five people lost their lives. The total cost of the disaster was NZ$40 billion—to this day, the centre of Christchurch has not been fully rebuilt. Australia's newspapers seemed to reel from the destruction in Brisbane to the catastrophe in Christchurch in a two-month-long rollercoaster of despair.

But there was another event that summer, just as geographically proximate to our lives in Australia, which barely rated a single line of newsprint. Daru is an island that lies off Papua New Guinea's southern coast, in Western Province. The distance between Daru and the closest part of Australia—Boigu Island—is just 110 kilometres. Between November 2010 and January 2011, Daru experienced a terrible outbreak of cholera, a water-borne disease that is prevalent in poverty-stricken places suffering from poor sewerage and water quality. The outbreak cost the lives of 300 people. And we didn't even notice.

Nothing more strikingly highlights the developmental challenges of the Pacific, and the radical difference in life's expectations determined by the lottery of being born in the greater Pacific compared with being born in Australia, than the cholera outbreak in Daru. It speaks to recurring human tragedies that we almost never acknowledge: tragedies in Betio, the Carteret Islands, Funafuti, and the list goes on. It speaks to how our immediate region is on the verge of having the worst set of quality-of-life indicators on the planet. And this is happening against the backdrop of global climate change. Behind every one of the statistics are real people suffering real hardships.

Australia is rightly judged by its actions in the Pacific. And we are at a crossroads as to whether that judgement will be favourable. It is imperative that Australia stands up and leads in the Pacific, for the sake of the ten million people who call it home.

ACKNOWLEDGEMENTS

Thank you to Louise Adler for giving me the opportunity to put my passion for the Pacific into print, and to Paul Smitz for copyediting this book.

Thank you to Kate Seward and Lidija Ivanovski for their help in proofing and editing this work.

My thanks to former prime minister Kevin Rudd for his generosity in opening the door to the Pacific to me.

Thanks to former prime minister Julia Gillard for giving me the opportunity to serve as the parliamentary secretary for Pacific island affairs and then as the parliamentary secretary for foreign affairs, and also to former foreign minister Bob Carr for his wise words.

At the risk of singling anyone out during my time working alongside DFAT, Jennifer Rawson was invaluable: what she doesn't know about the Pacific isn't worth knowing. Can I also pay tribute to all the professional DFAT staff whose knowledge of the Pacific is an incredible asset to our nation.

My travels would not have been possible without the logistical magic of the wonderful Saverina Chirumbolo.

And lastly and most importantly, thanks to my wonderful family for letting me travel: Rachel, my wife, and Sam, Bella, Harvey and Georgia. I love you all dearly.

NOTES

1   Pacific Islands Forum Secretariat, *2015 MDGs Tracking Report*,
    https://www.forumsec.org/wp-content/uploads/2020/03/2015-
    Pacific-Regional-MDGs-Tracking-Report.pdf (viewed February
    2021).

2   Edmund Barton, 1898 Australasian Federation Conference, Third
    Session, Debates, Melbourne, 21 January, https://parlinfo.aph.
    gov.au/parlInfo/download/constitution/conventions/1898-1093/
    upload_binary/1898_1093.pdf;fileType=application%2Fpdf#
    search=%22constitution/conventions/1898-1130%22 (viewed
    February 2021).

3   Australia-Japan Research Project, 'Remembering the War in New
    Guinea', http://ajrp.awm.gov.au/ajrp/remember.nsf/Web-Printer/
    58EBD6D993E15CE8CA256D05002671FD?OpenDocument
    (viewed February 2021). In addition, approximately 3500
    Australian soldiers were wounded, and 15 575 received treatment
    for disease: see Paul Ham, *Kokoda*, Harper Collins, 2005, p. 517.

4   This passage was adapted from a speech I made to the Lowy
    Institute in Sydney on 21 November 2017.

5   Pacific Islands Forum Secretariat, *2015 MDGs Tracking Report*.

6   John Vince, 'Millennium Development Goals: Progress in
    Oceania', *Archives of Disease in Childhood*, vol. 100, 2015,
    pp. S63–S65.

7   Ibid. In Vince's report, the PNG figure was given as US$35–
    US$40. The Australian Institute of Health and Welfare gives
    Australia's figure as A$5881: see Australian Institute of Health

and Welfare, 'Health Expenditure Australia 2011–12', 2013, https://www.aihw.gov.au/getmedia/6b21b4dc-5fd6-4077-8c75-7a6bab09416d/15405.pdf.aspx?inline=true (viewed February 2021).

8   Ibid. The figure given was 18 per cent.

9   Pacific Islands Forum Secretariat, *2015 MDGs Tracking Report*.

10 Vince, 'Millennium Development Goals'.

11 Statistics Division, Department of Economic and Social Affairs, United Nations, 'Millennium Development Goals: 2015 Progress Chart', 2015, http://mdgs.un.org/unsd/mdg/Resources/Static/Products/Progress2015/Progress_E.pdf (viewed February 2021).

12 Pacific Islands Forum Secretariat, *2015 MDGs Tracking Report*.

13 Australian Government, '2017 Foreign Policy White Paper', 2017, https://www.dfat.gov.au/publications/minisite/2017-foreign-policy-white-paper/fpwhitepaper/index.html (viewed February 2021).

14 Alexandre Dayant, 'Follow the Money: How Foreign Aid Spending Tells of Pacific Priorities', *The Interpreter*, 17 April 2019, https://www.lowyinstitute.org/the-interpreter/follow-money-how-foreign-aid-spending-tells-pacific-priorities (viewed February 2021).

15 Australian Government, '2017 Foreign Policy White Paper', p. 99.

16 Ibid.

17 Marcus Stephen, 'On Nauru, A Sinking Feeling', *The New York Times*, 18 July 2011.

18 Jamie Tahana, 'Australian PM's Attitude "Neo-colonial" Says Tuvalu', Radio New Zealand, 20 August 2019, https://www.rnz.co.nz/international/pacific-news/396972/australian-pm-s-attitude-neo-colonial-says-tuvalu (viewed February 2021).

19 ANU edge and The University of the South Pacific, *2013 SIG RAMSI People's Survey Report*, 26 June 2013, https://www.ramsi.org/wp-content/uploads/2014/07/FINAL-Peoples-Survey-2013-1-final-111900c1-79e2-4f41-9801-7f29f6cd2a66-0.pdf (viewed February 2021).

20   Holly Lawton, 'Australia's Seasonal Worker Program Now Bigger than New Zealand's', Devpolicy Blog, 25 July 2019, https://devpolicy.org/australias-seasonal-worker-program-now-bigger-than-nzs-20190725 (viewed February 2021).

21   World Bank Group, 'Maximizing the Development Impacts from Temporary Migration: Recommendations for Australia's Seasonal Worker Programme', 2017, http://documents1.worldbank.org/curated/en/572391522153097172/pdf/122270-repl-PUBLIC.pdf (viewed February 2021).

22   Ibid.

23   Australian Aid Tracker, 'Destinations: Which Countries Receive Our Aid, and How Our Aid Flows Are Changing', 2021, http://devpolicy.org/aidtracker/destinations/ (viewed February 2021).

24   Department of Foreign Affairs and Trade, *Aid Program Performance Report 2015–16: Papua New Guinea*, September 2016, https://www.dfat.gov.au/sites/default/files/papua-new-guinea-appr-2015-16.pdf (viewed February 2021).

25   Bruce Hill, 'Samoan PM Hits Back at Australia's "Insulting" Criticism of China's Aid Program in the Pacific', ABC News, 12 January 2018, https://www.abc.net.au/news/2018-01-12/samoan-prime-minister-hits-back-at-insulting-china-aid-comments/9323420 (viewed February 2021).

IN THE NATIONAL INTEREST

Other books on the issues that matter: